Dennis Hans Ladener

Philosophy made in Germany

Arthur Schopenhauer
A "little" introduction

Freethinkers

1st edition
© 2020 Dennis Hans Ladener
(dladener@googlemail.com)

Production and publishing: BoD - Books on Demand, Norderstedt.

ISBN: 9783751955263

Dennis Hans Ladener,
born May 11th, 1990
in Cologne/Germany,
is a German
philosopher and writer
who, at the young age
of only **29**, managed
to bring *eighteen*

"philosophical non-fiction books"
to market on his own.

The focus of his work, as well as
his thinking, is based on the
philosophy of the brilliant German
philosopher Arthur Schopenhauer
(* February 22, 1788 in Danzig;
† September 21, 1860 Frankfurt
am Main).

Since his main work
"The world as will and idea",

always had the greatest source of inspiration for himself.

"I must have always been a little weird, and even as a child I spent a lot of time thinking about the world. Fantasy, imagination and a strong natural curiosity have always been my most loyal companions. "

"The secret behind why I have become what I am is probably hidden in the fact that I have always avoided becoming an" adult "!"

In 2011, he successfully completed his three-year training as a **"Specialist for protection and security".**

From now on he could concentrate fully on his "personal study" of philosophy.

"At the age of 20, I finally fell in love with philosophy and finally with Arthur Schopenhauer's world of thought."

"It was a long, lonely and rocky road. But I've never regretted going with him! "

*The drive our author lies in dealing with complex and difficult to understand "philosophical", "socially critical" and "scientific" topics as simple and clear as possible to make it accessible to the general public.

Not an easy undertaking. But one that is definitely worth trying!

"But life is short and that Truth seems distant and lives a long time: let's tell the truth. "
~ *Arthur Schopenhauer*
* 1788-1860 †

Contents

Arthur Schopenhauer

Born in Danzig in 1788, died in
Frankfurt am Main in 1860, was an
outsider among philosophers.
He did not belong to any particular
school but bravely opposed the
dominant schools of thought of his
time by taking a more physical,
oriented philosophical path.

Human spirit, world history,
Meaning and goal, all of these are
illusions for him. For him the
world is a senseless stage play of
violence and agony.

Man ruled by irrational instincts
that World history without any
purpose, without any meaningful
development.
Life means suffering!

Schopenhauer studied in Göttingen and Berlin and received his doctorate in Jena in 1813. His doctoral thesis was his writing: "About the fourfold root of the principle of sufficient reason".

Compared to most other enlighteners and idealists, Schopenhauer was not a philosopher permeated with optimism, but rather a die-hard pessimist and misanthropist.

"Everything in life announces that earthly happiness is destined for it foiled or much worse than an illusion to be recognized."

"Life presents itself as a continued deception, in small things as well as in

Great, it promised so it won't keep unless to show how the desired was not desirable."

"Our world is the worst of all Worlds and something that shouldn't be better!"

"If a god made this world, I don't want to be that god. Her Sorrow would tear my heart apart. "

Schopenhauer's sympathy was, however, directed more towards animals than towards people.

He just didn't think much of his fellow men. So he remained an outsider not only in the philosophical but also in the social area.

Schopenhauer lived out of conviction and self-protection, but on the whole a rather lonely life.

"As long as you always have a right distanced relationship to your fellow human beings, one is not wounded by them, nor defiled and can endure it."

"Viewed in this way, society can be compared to a fire in which the Smart one warms himself some distance away but never reaches in directly like a booby."

It is therefore not particularly surprising that Schopenhauer was hardly interested in cultivating many friendships and remained both married and childless.

"To marry means to do what is possible to become a cornerstone of each other, his Halving rights and doubling one's duties."

Schopenhauer suffered massively from the world and from people, but this suffering about the world made him such a brilliant philosopher in the first place.

"Life is an awkward thing. I have set it up for myself to think about the same. "

The fruits of this reflection finally made him the most important thinker of modern times.

Schopenhauer, however, suffered from recurring depression and anxiety.

An annoying plague that should be with him for his entire life.

His only loyal companion was always a royal poodle, which he always called *Atman, the Sanskrit word for "breath of life", "Breath"*.

The ancient Indian writings of the **Upanishads** played a major role in Schopenhauer's worldview and philosophy.

The Upanishads speak of the essence of the inner self that is inherent in each of us and is the same in each one.

Or also from the individual soul "Atman" as part of "Brahman", the great world soul.

Whenever Schopenhauer's current Poodle died at what Life expectancy of poodles is likely to have been the case every 10 to 15 years, he immediately acquired a similar-looking poodle.

Schopenhauer was of the philosophical view that every dog contains every other dog at the same time.

In some anecdotes about Schopenhauer it is claimed that he had his poodle with him whenever he was naughty **"You human"** insulted.

Schopenhauer drew his knowledge from several basic pillars, on the one hand he was very fond of

"Plato's", "Immanuel Kant" and "Buddha's" philosophy
Interested, on the other hand he was also fascinated by ***"the Vedas" to be precise "The Upanishad".***

Vedas Sanskrit, m., वेद, veda,

"Knowledge", "holy doctrine" is a collection of religious texts in Hinduism that was first handed down orally and later written down.

The Upanishad उपनिषद्,

upaniṣad, f., Literally "to sit down in the vicinity", means "to sit at the feet of a teacher (guru)", 700 and 200 BC. Are a collection of philosophical Hindu scriptures and part of the Veda (late Veda period).

His main work ***"The world as will and imagination"*** was written in Dresden between 1814 and 1818 and was published in December 1818 with the year 1819 by Brockhaus in Leipzig.

Arthur Schopenhauer dies on September 21, 1860 in Frankfurt am Main at the age of 72 from pneumonia.

The world as an idea

Arthur Schopenhauer once asked himself what will become of the objects of the world if there is no one to perceive them?

The world we live in is full of objects, made by you as the subject.

A subject is characterized by the fact that it can perceive something of its surroundings in some way.

With you as a person, this happens through your five different ones "Tools of knowledge", colloquially also called "sense organs".

"See with the eyes"
"Hear with your ears"

"Smell with your nose"
"Taste with the tongue and the nose"
"Feel with the skin"

Each of these 5 sensory organs transmits information from the outside world to you in the form of electrical impulses Brain further.

For example, if you take a look around your surroundings, you will certainly be struck by numerous objects, which you can only perceive visually because a ray of light was previously reflected back in their direction by these objects.

When a beam of light hits an object, it saves the information about that object.

If the said light beam comes back into your eyes due to the reflection, the information contained in the light is passed on to your brain in this way.

The brain now has its own area for each of your senses, where the information received from the outside world is processed and interpreted.

The decisive factor here is the knowledge that the information from the outside world is not perceived, processed and interpreted in a completely identical manner by every living being.

This means that we as human beings by and large all experience an at least similarly uniform representation of the world, but it is This world perceived by us humans never "the world", since, due to the mutual interaction of subject and object, at no time can one assume a completely uniform version of the world.

There are an estimated 8 million different animal species on our planet, each of which is endowed with completely different and unique sense organs.

Even if they often appear to be very similar to our own sense organs, they nonetheless remain individual and therefore transmit the information from the outside world to the brain of the respective living being in a unique way.

The brains of the different life forms on our planet are by no means identical, but are unique for each species, which means that each living being experiences its own, very personal "idea" of a world.

The world that you experience every day is not the one and only world, but solely your own personal idea of a world and you experience it as it is possible for you as a person to experience it and not as it actually is, since this "actual" reality cannot exist at all but always only an idea of a world through a subject.

All the properties that you ascribe to things in the world exist only for you as a human being.

Colors which you e.g. perceive, can appear completely different to other living beings.

In this case, it depends entirely on how the eyes of the respective subject are constructed and thus how they transmit the data from the "outside world" to the brain.

The interaction of the most varied of sensory organs, in connection with the most varied of brains, generates the most varied of ideas about a world, but none of which is really the right one!

To claim the objects and Properties of the world could therefore exist for themselves, is therefore a big mistake, since the prerequisite for these would not be given in that case **"the subject"**.

The world, as you are used to it, never exists independently of your observation because this is not possible at all due to the laws of subject and object, but if you perceive the world, then only as it is possible for you as a human subject, to perceive them.

The ONE and ONLY world cannot exist, as every living being experiences a very personal idea of a world.

Schopenhauer's question, which seems strange at first, what is left of the world when no one is there to perceive it, is much more reasonable than previously assumed.

In addition, the question of the existence of reality was not his only problem, but he was also confronted with the misery that as a person he could only experience one of an inexpressibly many versions of a reality.

A dilemma that can only be overcome if you understand your next consideration that the human being is subject and object at the same time!

Our own body, says Schopenhauer, is basically nothing more than just one object among objects.

But it is the only object to which we have direct access, namely a kind of inner perspective.

It is true that one's own body is at least externally subject to the relationship between subject and object, which means that we can only perceive this as it is possible for us as humans to perceive it.

But at the same time we are also the subject and thus what knows.

Schopenhauer assumed that if you analyze your own inner goings-on, you can also speculate on the inner being of every other object and that you would have to understand what the world is independent of personal perception.

He described the result of his research in just one word: "Will"

And because the world, apart from this hidden will, can always only be an idea, he named the title of his main work:

"The world as will and idea."

What Schopenhauer wanted to express with this little word will is of course not completely clear at first.

The world as will

For him, the will is the driving force behind all phenomena in the world.

It is a will to exist, a will to live, a completely natural and original force which creates a world out of itself.

The entire universe would thus be merely an expression of the will and all objects within it, its individual manifestations.

With Schopenhauer, the will is the driving force behind all appearances of existence.

A force that keeps the world going and of which it is the origin.

Basically one could even claim that the will is Schopenhauer's interpretation of God, whereby this God, however, *is a blind, aimless driving force which one would rather compare with a reflex or an impulse.*

So everything that exists would be included You and me, an Objectified Manifestation of that Will Interpretation.

The will unconsciously creates itself out of itself in order to then be able to experience itself in the most varied of versions of itself.

However, this does not happen in a consciously willed and planned act of creation, but without a real goal, plan or control.

The will as the original force is always blind and aimlessly active with Schopenhauer, but it can become conscious of itself within its objectified manifestations.

In its objectified human form, the will can e.g. To really watch his own blind goings-on for the first time and, thanks to philosophy and natural sciences, even begin to recognize and understand his own being more and more.

The dual nature of man

Just like every other living being, humans are dependent on their "sense organs" in order to be able to experience something about the world.

What is special about humans, however, is that they are both subject and object at the same time, which means that our body represents an object among objects, but we are also the subject at the same time and thus what perceives.

Our own body is therefore the only object among all objects, in addition, due to our dual nature (subject and object), we can experience a direct, immediate inner perspective.

This does not mean that we can experience our own body independently of an idea.

But… it means that we are an object that can "experience" itself.

We have the possibility, so to speak, of studying the inner being of an object, namely our own "I", our needs, instincts and desires.

You will quickly find out that this "inner being" is your inner being, very similar to the beings in the entire world, and is actually one and the same being.

Humans themselves are therefore ideally suited to experiencing and researching their own inner being without any measuring devices, so we should ultimately be able to deduce the inner being of every other object based on the knowledge thus obtained.

The essence of the world is will!

Plants, animals and people have a lot more in common than some people would like to admit.

Every plant basically wants to start with taken "EXIST" grow exist and it would like to contribute to the preservation of the species.

Aside from that, however, their existence is pure existence.

• She has no real meaning in life even though she is alive.
• She lives to live alone.
• Her purpose was already fulfilled at the moment of her "EXISTENS".

The possible argument on your part that plants serve as food for many living beings and produce oxygen, I unfortunately cannot accept in this case, since these have not adapted to us (the living beings) but we have adapted to them (the plants).

With the animals, it hardly looks any different ...

"to adjust"
"to survive"
"eat"
"Propagate"

Every animal has to fulfill these tasks in the course of its otherwise pointless existence.

Due to our way of thinking that is far too romantic, we often overlook how terrible nature really is.

"Eat or be eaten".

The survival of the strongest, smartest or most adaptable is the motto there.

Already here there are clear signs of the meaninglessness and contradiction of life.

"Every living being can only exist by consuming another."

It makes no difference whether it is a plant, an animal or a human being. In nature there is no place for mercy if you want to persist in it.

All living beings are always trying to find a state of contentment for themselves to generate this means.

"Avoid pain"
"Generate satisfaction".

In the entire animal kingdom, this is best shown in the conservation of the species and the procurement of feed.

Every animal would literally do anything to avoid starvation, to reproduce and to protect itself and the offspring.

Animals do this because it is their destiny to do so. For them there is no further meaning in their life, this can be seen particularly well in their otherwise quite lazy attitude towards life.

If an animal is full and its body and its reproduction are not seriously endangered, it does nothing else, except "play" and "lounge around".

Basically, humans are nothing more than animals. Therefore our tasks are initially the same as with the animals.

> *"to adjust"*
> *"to survive"*
> *"eat"*
> *"Propagate".*

But of course, humans are no ordinary animals, because nothing on this planet is as unique as we humans.

• *Humans are probably the most complex living beings on this planet.*

• *We have learned to rearrange the world around us according to our needs.*

• *If we want to and if allowed, we can be an incredibly highly intelligent and sensitive being.*

• *Man has already accomplished innumerable great and cruel inventions and discoveries.*
• *We have even traveled to space.*

• *We learn from the past and plan our future.*

• We strive for status, recognition, fame, power, money and eternal youth.

• We want to own so much, although we hardly have any real use of it.

• We have feelings, feel love, happiness, joy, suffering, sadness, hate, greed, and anger.

• We are so multifaceted, we take on a different role at every moment in our life, we change "every day, every hour and every minute anyway.

• We start a family, raise our children, and later look after our parents.

• *We think about death and brood about the meaning of life - even gods we create ourselves.*

• *We philosophized and discovered science.*

"But most of us never really came to our senses!"

What humans, animals and plants definitely have in common is "willing".

The "existence" of every living being is determined by a will!

First of all, it is "the will to exist" which ensures that an unimaginable number of atoms are put together to form such a complex structure as a plant, an animal or us humans.

Within the manifested forms of the Willing to exist, "the will of pleasure" begins to rule.

This ensures that all manifestations always try to generate a state of contentment. However, the way in which they do this can be very different.

Finally, there is "the will to renew".

The will to renewal ensures the pronounced reproductive instinct of the manifestations, moreover it is the death of everyone, because it starts the aging process.

Because of this, there is a natural balance between life and death.

Life means suffering!

Because man is subject and object at the same time, he can experience the will that determines his existence for himself!

It is our desires, instincts and cravings that reflect the will and move us to drive.

With the existence / birth the "want" arises. "Suffering" arises through willing.

Here, too, the contradiction of life shows itself!

"With the birth comes the want and through this the suffering."

This is because we can never fully meet all of our needs. And even if we should succeed in doing this, after a very short time, a new number of these affectionate pests immediately emerge.

"Hence the problem of suffering is based on our wanting at all."

They are our unsatisfied ones Dreams, goals, desires and hopes that cause suffering in us and are triggered by the stubborn impulse of will which seems to be the true essence of the world.

**"Life means wanting.
To want means to suffer. "**

In order to be able to reduce the suffering, it is absolutely necessary to negate life and thus also the will to a very high degree.

This means giving up all attachment to this present existence and seeing through life itself as the real cause of all suffering.
Basically, it's pretty simple ...

Suffering always arises when something doesn't go the way we'd like it to. It is therefore important to learn to reduce one's own instinct to want to a minimum until it only prevails to the extent that the basic needs are guaranteed. That would be: eat, drink, sleep, and find safe accommodation.

Everything else in this life is first and foremost an optional * luxury

that is not absolutely necessary,
which I can treat myself to as
much as I can, but this must never
extend into a form of "attachment".

* With luxury in this case not only
the luxury of any material objects
is meant, but also the luxury of
dreams, goals, wishes and hopes.

This may all seem a bit excessive,
but in my opinion there are no
alternatives.

**"If you don't want anything, you
can't suffer either!"**

The whole secret is already in this
simple sentence and I think it is
not unfounded, which is why I
always imagine the life of a

simple, humble monk in this context.

The secret of a happy life is to approach it without any expectation. Modesty and discipline are key to this path.

You have reached your goal when even the smallest details in life bring you the greatest possible fulfillment.

This can be a simple sip of water, a fresh summer breeze, a chat, or a simple walk in nature. **Everything that brings you fulfillment without wanting to possess or control it can never harm you.**

However, if exactly these urges arise in you, I can only advise you to avoid the trigger as much as possible.

With this lifestyle, which may at first seem a little exaggerated, please consider that everyone has to decide for themselves how far they are willing to go for their own freedom.

Of course, from my own experience, I am very well aware of how difficult it can be to avoid what is initially good on the surface, but on closer analysis can be revealed as the cause of suffering. No matter how you decide now, the following insight will certainly remain:

**"With life comes wanting.
With wanting comes suffering!"**

Art "enjoyment without possession"

"Man is the only form of life on this planet that has it is granted to create works of art as well as to enjoy them."

Regardless of whether it is e.g. Statues, paintings, music or other art is, every single thing created by these people can produce unique feelings and powers in us.

Now let's begin to see the unique power of art.

Level 1. "Lower art" [Concrete] statues and paintings

The first stage of art is that

"Concrete Art". This means that the paintings and statues of this type were derived from what the respective creator of them could use from the world as a "natural model".

For a painting this could e.g. be a "natural landscape with animals" or a "basket of fruits".
In the case of a statue, e.g. a "Human" or "Animal".

For this reason, concrete art belongs to the lower art. But that shouldn't lessen their beauty.

The artist shouldn't be talked badly here either, because an enormous talent is required here too to cast a magical spell on the viewer of the work of art.

"Concrete art" makes it possible Objectifications of the will, that is "Our idea of the world", captured in the form of works of art and represented in this way.

Level 2. "Higher Art" [Abstract] statues and paintings

The second level of art is "abstract art". This is a "higher art" because it uses the forms that occur in the world, but the way in which these are captured in the respective work of art is a pure manifestation of the inner imagination of the respective artist.

The special thing here is that one and the same work of art can appear different to each viewer, this is because it is not immediately clear what the artist wanted to express with it.

If somebody tries to recognize exactly this anyway, the viewer literally has to look into the soul of the work or just create "his own interpretation" and thus "imagine" the work of art.

"Abstract art" also uses the templates of the world, but does not adopt them 1: 1, but only works with their "forms".

How these forms are ultimately implemented as a work of art is determined by the artist's "inner images" (ideas).

"However, these inner images arise just like thoughts, without any Control and out of nothing."

The special thing here is that the will in its manifested form as a human being creates another manifestation of itself in the form of an abstract work of art, its origin "The inner spiritual images" of the Artist and thus of the "will" itself.

Level 3. "Highest Art" The music

The third level of art is that "Music". This can be described as the "highest art" because, unlike the previously mentioned arts, "there are no natural models in nature".

This means that music literally begins to arise out of nothing, it can therefore be described as art, which in the real sense is nothing more than another variant of the objectification of the will.

The unique thing here, however, is that this takes place without "nature's template" and is therefore special can be called "pure".

"That is why music has the most influence on us compared to other works of art, because its powers are based on the purity of their objectivation stronger than that of the other arts."

"Music is an echo of the will itself, so it leaves us with the will and

Experience its expression directly and with a very high level of purity."

"The music" is also one of the many ways in which the will to show oneself is possible. What is special here, however, is that the will does not do this with music in the form of a "material body" and that it does not occur naturally in nature in its manifestation as music, but only from an already existing embodiment of the will "to man" out begins to arise.

Despite all the differences between the mentioned and not mentioned arts, they still have certain similarities, the effect of which on us is clearly recognizable.

Art is something that we can enjoy without immediately wanting to "own" it.

A work of art ensures that we can suspend "the illusion of separation" for a certain moment, because in order to be able to really understand art, the one who desires this has to become completely one with it.

He can't pretend he's there for One himself and towards himself is "the work of art", no, in order to understand art and produce its unique effect, he and the respective work of art must "form a complete and identical unit".

"Art enables us to have two elements that actually only

*emerge after the higher one
Knowledge was gained."*

On the one hand to enjoy something, or to find it beautiful and desirable without wanting to own it right away, and on the other hand to abolish the illusion of difference.

"The disadvantage here, however, is that art only succeeds in this for short-term moments, while higher knowledge also succeeds in the long-term View enables."

Art is "the little sister" of higher knowledge, just like with "Compassion" enables us to "intuitively" recognize certain connections, at least for a short time.

In order to taste this foretaste of higher knowledge, it is not absolutely necessary to focus on man-made art, because with a clear and alert look, all of nature can be recognized as a "gigantic work of art!

The best example is probably a sunrise or sunset or a rainbow.

Nature offers so many things that one could enjoy without the thought of "owning" and with which one can become a perfect one at the moment of enjoyment "Unity" can merge.

Most people have simply forgotten how to recognize this naturally given beauty!

Man cannot want what he wants!

"Man can do what he wants but not decide what he wants."

Schopenhauer's statement that one cannot want what one wants bears a resemblance to the teaching of **Buddha: The "acts done without a doer".**

A realization that brain research is slowly beginning to understand.

In summary, it means that the history of the world goes on without anyone being behind it.

Your alleged "actions", "thoughts" and "feelings" are not produced by you, but they simply arise and are only "experienced" by you.

This creates an illusion of supposedly "free" will. Basically, however, you are "consciousness" and thus the element that "experiences".

• *Thoughts arise without you doing anything.*
• *Feelings arise without your influence.*
• *Actions happen without your conscious participation.*

This can be seen particularly clearly in meditation, as this should basically always lead to increased awareness so that the meditator can be more clearly aware that he is not the voice that prevails in his head. And that all thoughts just buzz around and are not consciously generated.

On this way one also notices that all feelings and actions also just happen and that you want to do so without you consciously. As mentioned before, as a human being you are a "manifestation" of this blind force called will.

A force which is blind and aimless in its origin, but which can become fully aware of itself in its appearances.

Humans are particularly well suited to this (at least a few).

As soon as you realize that you are part of this world, but that you are only observing your existence, you stop identifying yourself with thoughts, feelings, and actions.

From then on, it's like watching a movie every day.

A film that simulates a life ... "your" life!

At this point, the Will in you, that is the force that you are in reality, see through your own blind goings-on and finally turn against yourself.

If you train enough mindfulness, you will more and more often slip into the position of the "pure observer" and not only that, you will become more and more clever at analyzing the events you have experienced in order to understand their connections.

After every experienced, allegedly freely executed action, you automatically reflect on its origin in order to understand the program sequence, which was behind it.

It is similar with thoughts and feelings, but this training requires... basically uninterrupted daily practice and concentration.

Once the will has seen through itself, it is free and can from now on decide for itself which feelings, thoughts and actions it lets itself into and which it learns to control by ignoring them in a controlled manner.

Of course, you can simply give yourself up to it completely and identify yourself with all events and dramas, or you can decide for yourself when you want to go into it "Lose" and when you will "check".

Once you have seen yourself through, the will, i.e. you, can reverse its essence and negate life itself.

He has thus recognized his blind madness and from now on knows how to suppress and turn around his own being. He thus withdraws from his own control, which allows him a completely new level of freedom and self-control.

Monks are a very good example of this, they learn to curb and understand themselves, are modest, already satisfied with the bare minimum and also live a life full of sacrifice for the service of all living beings.

You have seen through life itself as the cause of volition. And thus found the way to salvation while restraining yourself.

The extra sacrifice for everything Living ones, follow through her Unity thinking. For them everything forms a cosmic unit, where every form of life is worth the same.

With Schopenhauer this is Concept of unity based on

that it is the one and only will which creates the world out of itself and at the same time experiences itself in all its manifestations.

For Schopenhauer, **everything was one,** as if one were to claim that everything that exists, i.e. the entire universe, is actually God. Thus every living being would be a manifestation and thus an expression of God.

But according to Schopenhauer, this god is a blind and haphazard god who cannot control his power and only experiences in his manifestation what he is doing himself!

Compassionate ethics

"The delusion of egoism can be resolved through pity."

"By empathizing with others and making their suffering my own at the same time, the suffering of the Encourage others to help him."

Through this zest for action, "the illusion of me and you" is lifted for a very short but sufficient moment.

"But caution is advised!"

Because "true compassion" is only really given when the resulting deeds are free from any "praise and / or reward thoughts".

The unique power of compassion comes from being "placed" in the situation of the other living being, regardless of whether it is a plant, animal or human.

"For him really Compassionate, suffering is the Others also own Suffering."

Living beings who truly feel "pure compassion" receive the power of "higher knowledge", although they have never heard of it.

Those who are filled with pity will no longer be able to hurt anyone, be indulgent, forgive and help wherever they can.

"A compassionate person always recognizes the suffering of others

as his own because he has recognized himself in all living beings and becomes one with them on this path."

When you meet other people, you shouldn't indulge in any prejudices, but theirs "Pain" and her "suffering" as well as hers Recognize "fears" and "hardships".

This way you will not only perceive the negative in them, rather...

... one reflects oneself in them and recognizes through the sympathy that one's own so familiar beings also in everyone else.

"Compassion is the unconscious

Self-knowledge of the will about its own being."

"In compassion, worries about your own existence take the place of everything Living."

Man alone has the ability to feel compassion for other living beings, so it should theoretically be possible for him to see his own beings in everything else and to act accordingly.

Does death mean the final end?

In this world, death only means the transition from one to the other; the old must constantly give way so that new characters can take their place on the stage of life.

God made for himself the theater stage, which we call the world or universe, must constantly change, destroy and renew so that it can fully fulfill its purpose.

The best possible multi-faceted simultaneous self-experience of the one and only God.

God does not benefit from incarnating initially in different living beings, but then for all of them Time has to reduce, limit and narrow down his experiences to the same.

Such an all-encompassing incomparable being like God can probably never reach a final stage where it has understood itself completely.

Your change and the one that comes with it Variety of their Manifestations seem to be almost infinite.

God uses himself like one Plasticine, which changes its appearance over and over again, but always consists of one and the same substance.

But even if this might mean that our personal self is actually lost after death, it should perhaps still be a very comforting thought for each of us that we should all find our way back in one way or another find in this world.

"Only this time in a different shape and without any memory of the previous one To be there."

But for many of us it is precisely this one thought, the greatest fear and worry. Most of them forget that there was an incredibly long period of time before they were born, at least. *I have not yet met anyone who spoke to me with concern about the time before their birth!*

But almost all people are horrified or even angry that after their death another period should take place without them.

Notes

Notes

Notes